by Pearl Markovics

Consultant:
Beth Gambro
Reading Specialist
Yorkville, Illinois

Contents

Pug Hug............................2

Key Words in the *-ug* Family.......16

Index.............................16

About the Author..................16

New York, New York

Pug Hug

Let's rhyme!

This is a little **bug**.

The **bug** is on a **mug**.

Here is a **jug**.
It is next to
the **mug**.

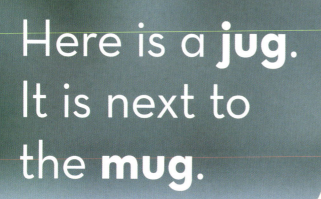

Crash!
The **jug** falls on the **rug**.

The crash scares the **pug**.

The **pug** gives my sock a **tug**.

I give my **pug** a big **hug**!

Key Words in the -ug Family

bug   **hug**   **jug**   **mug**

pug   **rug**   **tug**

Other **-ug** Words: **dug, lug, plug, snug**

Index

bug 2-3, 4-5   jug 6-7, 8-9   pug 10-11, 12-13, 14-15   rug 8-9
hug 14-15   mug 4-5, 6-7   tug 12-13

About the Author

Pearl Markovics enjoys having fun with words. She especially likes witty wordplay.

Teaching Tips

Before Reading
- ✓ Introduce rhyming words and the **-ug** word family to readers.
- ✓ Guide readers on a "picture walk" through the text by asking them to name the things shown.
- ✓ Discuss book structure by showing children where text will appear consistently on pages. Highlight the supportive pattern of the book.

During Reading
- ✓ Encourage readers to "read with your finger" and point to each word as it is read. Stop periodically to ask children to point to a specific word in the text.
- ✓ Reading strategies: When encountering unknown words, prompt readers with encouraging cues such as:
  - **Does that word look like a word you already know?**
  - **Does it rhyme with another word you have already read?**

After Reading
- ✓ Write the key words on index cards.
  - **Have readers match them to pictures in the book.**
- ✓ Ask readers to identify their favorite page in the book. Have them read that page aloud.
- ✓ Choose an **-ug** word. Ask children to pick a word that rhymes with it.
- ✓ Ask children to create their own rhymes using **-ug** words. Encourage them to use the same pattern found in the book.

Credits: Cover, © Anna Cinaroglu/Shutterstock; 2–3, © irini-k/Shutterstock; 4–5, © In Green/Shutterstock and © irini-k/Shutterstock; 6–7, © Tim UR/Shutterstock; 8–9, © RichardCH/Shutterstock and © Anthony Paz/Shutterstock; 10–11, © Jogodka/Shutterstock, © Pix11/Shutterstock, and © Anthony Paz/Shutterstock; 12–13, © Aseph/Shutterstock and © Africa Studio/Shutterstock; 14–15, © Anna Cinaroglu/Shutterstock; 16T (L to R), © irini-k/Shutterstock, © Anna Cinaroglu/Shutterstock, © Tim UR/Shutterstock, and © In Green/Shutterstock; 16B (L to R), © Jogodka/Shutterstock, © Anthony Paz/Shutterstock, and © Aseph/Shutterstock.

Publisher: Kenn Goin **Senior Editor:** Joyce Tavolacci **Creative Director:** Spencer Brinker

Library of Congress Cataloging-in-Publication Data: Names: Markovics, Pearl, author. | Gambro, Beth, consultant. Title: Pug hug / by Pearl Markovics; consultant: Beth Gambro, Reading Specialist, Yorkville, Illinois. Description: New York, New York: Bearport Publishing, [2020] | Series: Read and rhyme: Level 2 | Includes index. Identifiers: LCCN 2019007617 (print) | LCCN 2019012646 (ebook) | ISBN 9781642806014 (Ebook) | ISBN 9781642805475 (library) | ISBN 9781642807127 (pbk.) Subjects: LCSH: Readers (Primary) Classification: LCC PE1119 (ebook) | LCC PE1119 .M28575 2020 (print) | DDC 428.6/2—dc23 LC record available at https://lccn.loc.gov/2019007617

Copyright © 2020 Bearport Publishing Company, Inc. All rights reserved. No part of this publication may be reproduced in whole or in part, stored in any retrieval system, or transmitted in any form or by any means, electronic, mechanical, photocopying, recording, or otherwise, without written permission from the publisher. For more information, write to Bearport Publishing Company, Inc., 45 West 21 Street, Suite 3B, New York, New York, 10010. Printed in the United States of America.

10 9 8 7 6 5 4 3 2 1